Firestone, Mary

COMMUNITY HELPERS
SECURITY GUARDS

Security Guards

by Mary Firestone

Consultant:
Greg Endres
Senior Training Technician—Police
New York State Division of Criminal Justice

Bridgestone Books
an imprint of Capstone Press
Mankato, Minnesota

Bridgestone Books are published by Capstone Press
151 Good Counsel Drive, P.O. Box 669, Mankato, Minnesota 56002
http://www.capstone-press.com

Library of Congress Cataloging-in-Publication Data
Firestone, Mary.
  Security guards/Mary Firestone.
  v. cm. —(Community helpers)
  Includes bibliographical references and index.
  Contents: What security guards do—What security guards wear—Tools security guards
  use—What security guards drive—Security guards and school—Where security guards
  work—People who help security guards—How security guards help others.
  ISBN 0-7368-1616-X (hardcover)
  1. Police, Private—Juvenile literature. [1. Security guards. 2. Occupations.] I. Title.
  II. Community Helpers (Mankato, Minn.)
  HV8290 .F565 2003
  363.28'9—dc21   2002010709

Summary: A simple introduction to the work security guards do, discussing where they
  work, what tools they use, and how they are important to the community they serve.

Editorial Credits
Heather Adamson, editor; Karen Risch, product planning editor; Patrick D. Dentinger,
    cover production designer; Alta Schaffer, photo researcher

Photo Credits
CORBIS/AFP, 4, 20; SABA/Mark Peterson, 6; Reuters NewMedia, 8, 18; Phil Banko, 10;
    Neal Preston, 14; Ed Kash, 16
Index Stock Imagery/Jim McGuire, cover
Unicorn Stock Photos/Aneal Vohra, 12

1 2 3 4 5 6 08 07 06 05 04 03

Table of Contents

Security Guards

Security guards protect people and their belongings. They work at airports, banks, hotels, and sporting events. They watch for fires and help stop crime.

What Security Guards Do

Security guards watch shoppers and building visitors. They keep order at events and concerts. They check people at airports for dangerous items. Guards patrol areas to make them safe. They call the police if they see a crime.

patrol
to walk or drive by an area

What Security Guards Wear

Most security guards wear uniforms with a badge. Some dress in suits and ties. Some security guards wear bullet-proof vests. They sometimes carry clubs or guns.

Tools Security Guards Use

Security guards use equipment to protect people. They use scanners and metal detectors to find dangerous items. TV screens show who is entering and leaving a building. Some guards use guns to help stop crimes.

metal detector
a machine that can find metals

11

What Security Guards Drive

Some security guards use vehicles. They drive cars or motor scooters to patrol outdoor areas. They use armored vehicles to move large amounts of money. They also patrol on foot.

armor

a heavy metal layer that protects against bullets or bombs

Security Guards and School

Many security guards go to school to learn their jobs. They learn ethics, laws, and how to keep buildings safe. They learn how to use guns. They sometimes are trained at work by other guards.

ethics
deciding what is
the right thing to do

Where Security Guards Work

Security guards work in banks, office buildings, and hotels. They also work at shopping centers, sports events, and concerts. Some guards work in night clubs. They stop people who cause trouble.

People Who Help Security Guards

Many people help security guards. The police help when there is a crime. Other people help security guards by telling them if they see a problem. If there is a fire, security guards call firefighters to help them.

How Security Guards Help Others

Security guards help make the world a safer place. They protect people from theft, fires, and vandalism. They help people safely enjoy work, shopping, and other events.

vandalism
the wrecking of property

Hands On: Being Alert

Security guards must be alert. They watch everything around them for signs of danger. This game will help you practice watching and being alert.

What You Need

One or more friends
Notebooks
Pencils
A timer

What You Do

1. Give each player a notebook and a pencil.
2. Find an area where the players can sit down. It could be a room in the house or somewhere outside.
3. Set the timer for two minutes. Have someone start it and say, "Go!"
4. Players should write down everything they see and hear around them. Keep writing until the timer stops.
5. Compare lists. Who saw the most things? Who heard the most sounds? Who noticed the most interesting things? Move to another place and try the game again.

Words to Know

armor (AR-mur)—a heavy metal layer that protects against bullets or bombs; security guards sometimes drive armored vehicles.

metal detector (MET-uhl di-TEK-tur)—a machine that can find metals

patrol (puh-TROLE)—to walk or drive by an area; security guards patrol to watch for problems

scanner (SKAN-ehr)—a machine that looks very closely at objects to search for information or find problems

vandalism (VAN-duhl-ihzm)—the wrecking of property

Read More

Goldberg, Jan. *Security Guard.* Careers without College. Mankato, Minn.: Capstone Press, 1999.

Liebman, Daniel. *I Want to be a Police Officer.* Toronto, Ont.: Firefly Books, 2000.

Internet Sites

Track down many sites about security guards.
Visit the FACT HOUND at *http://www.facthound.com*

IT IS EASY! IT IS FUN!

1) Go to *http://www.facthound.com*
2) Type in: 073681616X
3) Click on "FETCH IT" and FACT HOUND will find several links hand-picked by our editors.

Relax and let our pal FACT HOUND do the research for you!

Index